Dynamic
Sermon
Outlines

Dynamic Sermon Outlines

Russell E. Spray

BAKER BOOK HOUSE
Grand Rapids, Michigan 49516

ISBN: 0-8010-8297-8

Third printing, November 1993

Printed in the United States of America

Contents

Foreword

Dynamic Sermon Outlines is designed to assist busy pastors with their sermon preparation. These outlines are easy to use and easy to remember. I pray that all who use and hear them will be blessed and God will be glorified.

Russell E. Spray

1

B-E-A-T Discouragement

"Why art thou cast down, O my soul? and why art thou disquieted within me? hope thou in God: for I shall yet praise him, who is the health of my countenance, and my God" (Ps. 43:5).

I. B-elieve the Promises of God
"Whereby are given unto us exceeding great and precious promises: that by these ye might be partakers of the divine nature . . ." (2 Peter 1:4).

A. When discouragement strikes, many Christians are tempted to doubt God's promises. They think they are written for others, not themselves.

B. God's Word assures us that the promises "were written for our learning, that we through patience and comfort of the scriptures might have hope" (Rom. 15:4).

C. Beat discouragement by believing God's promises. We must read them, reread them, and appropriate them for ourselves.

II. E-xpect the Presence of God
". . . I will never leave thee, nor forsake thee. . . . The Lord is my helper . . ." (Heb. 13:5-6).

A. When discouraged, some Christians do not feel his presence and are tempted to doubt God and their salvation.

B. Few, if any, Christians feel God's presence at all times. We must depend on our faith not feelings.

C. To win over discouragement, we must expect God's presence and rely on his promises. Jesus said, "Lo, I am with you alway, even unto the end of the world" (Matt. 28:20).

III. A-ccept the Peace of God
"And the peace of God, which passeth all understanding, shall keep your hearts and minds through Christ Jesus" (Phil. 4:7).

A. Many Christians fail to accept the peace God offers. They persistently hold to their negative and distressed attitudes.

B. Through deliberate action, negatives must be replaced with positives. Look for the good things in life, not the bad.

C. Jesus said, "Peace I leave with you, my peace I give unto you" (John 14:27). Beat discouragement by simply accepting his peace.

IV. T-riumph with Praise to God
"Hope in God: for I shall yet praise him . . ." (Ps. 43:5).

A. Most of us fail to praise the Lord as we should. When discouragement strikes, we mope in self-pity and despair.

B. Praise enables us to win over discouragement. The more we praise him, the greater victory we enjoy. Triumph by praising God.

C. The psalmist said, "But I will hope continually, and will yet praise thee more and more" (Ps. 71:14).

2

Burdens Are Lifted

"Cast thy burden upon the LORD, and he shall sustain thee: he shall never suffer the righteous to be moved" (Ps. 55:22).

God will lift the burdens of his children today.

I. The Surrendering

"Cast thy burden upon the LORD . . ." (Ps. 55:22).

A. Many Christians fail to cast their burdens upon the Lord. They try to carry them in their own strength and fail.

B. Some cast their burdens on the Lord but do not leave them with him. They continue to be crushed and overwhelmed.

C. Total surrender is needed. Our burdens must be left with the Lord. Finite strength fails but God's infinite power is all-sufficient.

D. Peter admonished, "Casting all your care upon him; for he careth for you" (1 Peter 5:7).

II. The Sustaining

". . . and he shall sustain thee" (Ps. 55:22).

A. Sustain means "to keep in existence; keep up . . . carry the weight or burden of . . . to strengthen the spirits . . . comfort . . . encourage"—Webster.

B. Many Christians do not appropriate God's sustaining grace, because they fail to trust him sufficiently.

C. Scripture says, "And the Lord shall help them, and deliver them . . . because they trust in him" (Ps. 37:40).

D. God sustains his trusting children. The psalmist wrote, "I laid me down and slept; I awakened; for the LORD sustained me" (Ps. 3:5).

III. The Stabilizing

"He shall never suffer the righteous to be moved" (Ps. 55:22).

A. Some Christians lack stability. They are wishy-washy, up one day and down the next.

B. If we please God, we must be steadfast, keeping the faith in the midst of trials, troubles, and testing.

C. God sometimes allows burdens to come to strengthen our faith. He lifts them as we trust and obey.

D. God's Word promises, "The God of all grace . . . after that ye have suffered a while, make you perfect, stablish, strengthen, settle you" (1 Peter 5:10).

3

Defining God's Mercy

"But the mercy of the LORD is from everlasting to everlasting upon them that fear him . . ." (Ps. 103:17).

I. Loving
"Hear me, O LORD; for thy lovingkindness is good: turn unto me according to the multitude of thy tender mercies" (Ps. 69:16).
A. Webster defines mercy as "a blessing that is an act of divine favor or compassion."
B. God's mercy is loving. He loved us while we were afar off, still in our sins, and without hope.
C. Because of God's loving mercy, he gave Jesus as a sacrifice for sin. Jesus gave himself to die in our place. ". . . Christ died for us" (Rom. 5:8).

II. Liberating
"If the Son therefore shall make you free, ye shall be free indeed" (John 8:36).
A. Many Christians are in bondage to their own selfish desires. They are also in bondage to the opinions of others.
B. God's mercy is liberating. It sets us free from self-centeredness and the opinions of people.
C. Jesus said, "And ye shall know the truth, and the truth shall make you free" (John 8:32).

III. Lifting
"But Jesus took him by the hand, and lifted him up; and he arose" (Mark 9:27).
A. Jesus had mercy on the father of the epileptic boy. He healed the afflicted son. He "lifted him up; and he arose."

B. God's mercy lifts people today. The drunkard, gambler, thief, prostitute, homosexual, and all who repent and forsake their sins may be lifted up.

C. God's Word promises, "If we confess our sins, he is faithful and just to forgive us our sins, and to cleanse us from all unrighteousness" (1 John 1:9).

IV. Lasting

"For the LORD is good; his mercy is everlasting; and his truth endureth to all generations" (Ps. 100:5).

A. Few things in today's world are lasting. The material goods of this world wear out, rust, decay, and soon disappear.

B. Many people build their hopes on temporal things. They cannot take them to the next life. All must be left behind.

C. God's mercy is everlasting. He is ever ready to forgive and cleanse those who come to him in simple, trusting faith (Ps. 136:1–26).

4

D-R-A-W Near to God

"Draw nigh to God, and he will draw nigh to you" (James 4:8).

Draw near to God by heeding the following points:

I. D-elight

"Delight thyself also in the LORD; and he shall give thee the desires of thine heart" (Ps. 37:4).

A. Some Christians are overly concerned about world conditions and their personal problems. Therefore, they fail to delight in the Lord.

B. We draw near to God when we put everything in his hands and trust him for the results.

C. The psalmist said, "I delight to do thy will, O my God: yea, thy law is within my heart" (Ps. 40:8).

II. R-ely

"Trust in the LORD with all thine heart; and lean not unto thine own understanding" (Prov. 3:5).

A. Many Christians rely on self-effort and fail. Some depend on other people more than God.

B. We draw near to God by relying on him for our strength. Our strength is finite, but God's power is infinite.

C. The psalmist admonished: "Commit thy way unto the LORD; trust also in him; and he shall bring it to pass" (Ps. 37:5).

III. A-chieve

"That ye might walk worthy of the Lord unto all pleasing, being fruitful in every good work . . ." (Col. 1:10).

A. Achieve means "to attain a desired end or aim—to become successful"—Webster.

B. Some Christians fear criticism or failure. Paul said, "I can do all things through Christ which strengtheneth me" (Phil. 4:13).

C. We draw near to God when we do his work, using our time, talent, and treasure to assist the less fortunate, comfort the bereaved, and console the sick and lonely.

IV. W-ait

"I waited patiently for the LORD; and he inclined unto me, and heard my cry" (Ps. 40:1).

A. Many Christians become impatient. They fail to wait upon the Lord because they want everything to happen at their appointed time.

B. God's timing is always best. He is never too early or too late. Waiting should be a time of drawing near to God.

C. Scripture says, "But they that wait upon the LORD shall renew their strength" (Isa. 40:31).

5

Dimensions of Christ's Love

"[That you] may have power, together with all the saints, to grasp how wide and long and high and deep is the love of Christ" (Eph. 3:18, NIV).

The aim of this message is to explore the vast dimensions of Christ's love.

I. The Breadth of Christ's Love

"May have power . . . to grasp how wide . . . is the love of Christ" (Eph. 3:18).

A. The love of many Christians is narrow in scope. It is limited to family, relatives, and a few friends. They fail to be the blessing they should be.

B. Christ's love is broader than the widest sea. His love includes all races, religions, and ranks—the whole world.

C. We must reach out in love also. We should include everyone—sick, lonely, needy, rich, great (1 John 4:9–11).

II. The Length of Christ's Love

"May have power . . . to grasp how . . . long . . . is the love of Christ" (Eph. 3:18).

A. The love of many Christians is short-lived. Their love is controlled by their emotions and rises or falls with their whims.

B. Christ's love is enduring and eternal. The Lord said, "I have loved thee with an everlasting love" (Jer. 31:3).

C. Christ doesn't love for just a day, week, month, or year, but he loves everlastingly.

III. The Height of Christ's Love

"May have power . . . to grasp how . . . high . . . is the love of Christ" (Eph. 3:18).

- A. The love of many Christians is limited. It is stymied by their own selfish motives and desires.
- B. There is no limit to the reach of Christ's love. It goes beyond the highest mountain, the moon, the sun, and the remotest star.
- C. Christ's love reaches the loftiest, the proud. He also lifts up those in the gutter, bringing both together, putting them on the same level in Christ Jesus (Rom. 3:23).

IV. The Depth of Christ's Love

"May have power . . . to grasp how . . . deep is the love of Christ" (Eph. 3:18).

- A. Christ's love goes deeper than the deepest sea. He loves with an infinite love.
- B. Christ's love reaches down and lifts up the discouraged, despondent, and depressed.
- C. Christ's love reaches down to humble sinners—prostitutes, homosexuals, murderers, thieves—all who come to him and forsake their sins (Mic. 7:19).

6

Essentials for God's W-O-R-K

"I must work the works of him that sent me, while it is day: the night cometh, when no man can work" (John 9:4).

I. Be W-illing to Work
"That they do good . . . ready to distribute, willing to communicate" (1 Tim. 6:18).

A. Many Christians fail to do God's work because of their unwillingness. They are busy seeking possessions and pleasure for themselves.

B. God's Word admonishes, "Set your affections on things above, not on things on the earth" (Col. 3:2).

C. We must desire to do God's work. We must be diligent and faithful to work "while it is day."

II. Be O-rganized for Work
"Let all things be done decently and in order" (1 Cor. 14:40).

A. Many Christians are without orderliness. They work haphazardly, lacking organization. Therefore, they fail.

B. Being organized eliminates confusion. Scriptures teach, "God is not the author of confusion" (1 Cor. 14:33).

C. Organization is essential. It brings purpose and unity and helps us accomplish God's work successfully.

III. Be R-eliable at Work
"The harvest truly is plenteous, but the labourers are few" (Matt. 9:37).

A. Some Christians do God's work spasmodically. They work only when they feel like it. They are undependable.

B. Scripture admonishes Christians to be dependable. "... that they which have believed in God might be careful to maintain good works" (Titus 3:8).

C. We must be reliable when doing God's work, for time is running out. Now is the opportunity because "the night cometh, when no man can work" (John 9:4).

IV. Be K-ind as You Work

"And be ye kind one to another, tenderhearted, forgiving one another ..." (Eph. 4:32).

A. Christians are sometimes unkind when doing God's work. A domineering attitude causes hurt and hinders his kingdom.

B. We must be kind, patient, and understanding, especially when doing service for the Lord, considering the feelings and rights of others (Col. 3:12).

7

Faith for Trying Times

"That the trial of your faith, being much more precious than of gold that perisheth, though it be tried with fire, might be found unto praise and honour and glory at the appearing of Jesus Christ" (1 Peter 1:7).

The following points offer Christians suggestions for coping in trying times.

I. Positive Faith
"That the trial of your faith . . ." (1 Peter 1:7).
- A. Temptation, testing, and trials come to all Christians. Positive faith is needed to win over the devil's onslaughts.
- B. Some Christians possess a negative attitude. They lack positive faith. When trials strike, they are overwhelmed.
- C. We must declare with the songwriter, "I can, I will, I do believe" even when the odds are against us (Mark 11:24).

II. Precious Faith
". . . being much more precious than of gold that perisheth . . ." (1 Peter 1:7).
- A. The Christian's faith is indeed "precious." ". . . without faith it is impossible to please him" (Heb. 11:6).
- B. Peter referred "to them that have obtained like precious faith with us through the righteousness of God . . ." (2 Peter 1:1).
- C. Faith is precious because it is of rare value. Nothing is more important than a personal faith in God. It is the answer for trying times and brings assurance of victory to God's people (1 John 5:4).

III. Persistent Faith

". . . though it be tried with fire . . ." (1 Peter 1:7).

A. Many Christians lack a persistent faith. When fiery trials strike, they throw up their hands in despair.

B. Scripture tells us to "hold fast the profession of our faith without wavering; (for he is faithful that promised)" (Heb. 10:23).

C. Persistent faith is needed for trying times. Whatever happens, we must keep on keeping on. Our faith will not fail us if we do not fail our faith.

IV. Praising Faith

". . . might be found unto praise and honour and glory at the appearing of Jesus Christ" (1 Peter 1:7).

A. Most Christians fail to praise the Lord enough. When trying times come, they praise him even less.

B. The psalmist said, "I will bless the Lord at all times: his praise shall continually be in my mouth" (Ps. 34:11).

C. Praising faith is needed in this life because it helps fit us for heaven where we shall praise the Lord eternally.

8

God Answers Our Prayers

"I waited patiently for the Lord; and he inclined unto me, and heard my cry" (Ps. 40:1).

God answered the psalmist's prayer. He answers our prayers also. Many things are accomplished through prayer.

I. The Regenerating

"He brought me up also out of an horrible pit, out of the miry clay . . ." (Ps. 40:2).

A. To be regenerated means to be "spiritually reborn—renewed or restored especially after a decline to a low or abject condition"—Webster.

B. When humankind sinned through disobedience to God, they became degenerated. Christ became our sacrifice. Through his atoning blood, we can become regenerated.

C. We must come to God just as we are, in simple trusting faith, repenting of our sins and believing on Jesus Christ.

II. The Reestablishing

". . . and set my feet upon a rock, and established my goings" (Ps. 40:2).

A. Many Christians become slack concerning spiritual matters. They fail to pray as they should. They neglect God's house and his Word. They need to be reestablished.

B. When we become less than we should be for God, we need to rededicate and recommit ourselves to him and let him reestablish us.

C. God's Word tells us to "present your bodies a living sacrifice, holy, acceptable unto God . . ." (Rom. 12:1).

III. The Rejoicing

"And he hath put a new song in my mouth, even praise unto our God . . ." (Ps. 40:3).

A. Some Christians are slack when it comes to rejoicing in the Lord. They take themselves too seriously and look for the bad in others and their circumstances.

B. Forgiven and cleansed Christians should praise the Lord continually, rejoicing always in him. They should look for the good in others and their circumstances.

C. The psalmist advised Christians to "be glad in the Lord, and rejoice, ye righteous: and shout for joy . . ." (Ps. 32:11).

IV. The Rewarding

". . . many shall see it, and fear, and shall trust in the Lord" (Ps. 40:3).

A. Christians should be ready to testify to the wonder-working power of God. They should exhibit joy that the world doesn't give and cannot take away.

B. When others see the joy of the Lord manifested in us, they will want him also.

C. The psalmist said, "Many shall see it . . . and shall trust in the Lord" (Ps. 40:3). This is our reward—when we see others come to the throne of grace and trust Christ, accepting him as their personal Savior and Lord.

9

God Watches over His Own

"The eyes of the Lord are upon the righteous, and his ears are open unto their cry" (Ps. 34:15).

Today's world is filled with danger, but God watches over his own.

I. Through Sincere Prayer
"Praying always with all prayer and supplication in the Spirit . . ." (Eph. 6:18).
- A. Many Christians are lax when it comes to praying for God's protective care. Perhaps they think they can make it on their own, but God wants us to take everything to him.
- B. God hears and answers sincere prayer. Let us pray for our personal safety, our loved ones' safety, our friends' safety, and for the safety of God's people everywhere.
- C. The psalmist said, "He shall call upon me, and I will answer him: I will be with him in trouble; I will deliver him, and honour him" (Ps. 91:15).

II. Through Scriptural Promises
"Whereby are given unto us exceeding great and precious promises" (2 Peter 1:4).
- A. God has given us many scriptural promises concerning his protective care. We should read them and claim them as our own.
- B. The psalmist said, "I will say of the Lord, He is my refuge and my fortress: my God; in him will I trust" (Ps. 91:2).
- C. Trust in the Lord. Believe his promises for safe keeping. They are "exceeding great and precious."

III. Through Sensible Precautions

"And the LORD shall . . . deliver them from the wicked, and save them because they trust in him" (Ps. 37:40).

A. Many Christians subject themselves to needless dangers both at home and away from home.

B. Some take foolish chances while driving cars. Others are careless about fire. They are haphazard and fail to practice safety measures at home.

C. God expects his people to take sensible precautions in today's dangerous society. We must do our best and trust God for the rest.

IV. Through Supernatural Providence

"For he shall give his angels charge over thee, to keep thee in all thy ways" (Ps. 91:11).

A. Providence: "Divine guidance . . . God, conceived as the power sustaining and guiding human destiny"—Webster.

B. While watching over his own, God may intervene directly. Sometimes he sends his angels to intervene for us. "For he shall give his angels charge over thee . . ." (Ps. 91:11–12).

Good **10**

How to Win over Stress

"Casting all your care upon him; for he careth for you" (1 Peter 5:7).

Christians can win over stress if they:

I. Learn from the Lord
"For whatsoever things were . . . written for our learning, that we through . . . the scriptures might have hope" (Rom. 15:4).
A. Many Christians do not meditate on God's Word as they should. They fail to learn from God.
B. The Bible is God's Word to us, written for our learning, comfort, and hope.
C. We can win over stress by finding the promises that fit our area of need, writing them down, remembering them, and claiming them as our own (2 Cor. 1:20).

II. Lean on the Lord
"Trust in the LORD with all thine heart; and lean not unto thine own understanding" (Prov. 3:5).
A. Some Christians fail to lean on the Lord in times of stress. They depend on their own power and fail.
B. Many people lean on counselors, doctors, lawyers, or friends. Their help is finite and temporal. God's help is infinite and never fails (Ps. 37:5).
C. To win over stress, we must trust the Lord without reserve. He promised, "Draw nigh to God, and he will draw nigh to you" (James 4:8).

III. Lift with the Lord
"For we are labourers together with God" (1 Cor. 3:9).

A. Some Christians are remiss when it comes to doing God's work. They are too busily engaged in personal pursuits.

B. Scripture teaches that God comforts us "that we may be able to comfort them which are in any trouble . . ." (2 Cor. 1:4).

C. Work is a good antidote for stress. Doing God's work is even more helpful. When we assist others unselfishly, we receive help for ourselves.

IV. Love as the Lord

"As the Father hath loved me, so have I loved you: continue ye in my love" (John 15:9).

A. Many Christians suffer stress because they lack love for God and others. Their lives are motivated by self-centeredness and materialistic pursuits.

B. We must surrender to God unreservedly and make a total commitment to him. His Holy Spirit will cleanse our hearts and fill us with God's love (1 Thess. 5:23).

11

How to Please God

"Make you perfect in every good work to do his will, working in you that which is wellpleasing in his sight, through Jesus Christ" (Heb. 13:21).

To be well pleasing in God's sight, we must:

I. Be Forgiving
". . . forgiving one another, even as God for Christ's sake hath forgiven you" (Eph. 4:32).
- A. Some Christians falter when it comes to forgiving others. They continue to hold ill feelings and resentments.
- B. We must forgive if we are to be pleasing to God. Even if people do not forgive us, we must forgive them.
- C. Scripture warns, "But if ye forgive not men their trespasses, neither will your Father forgive your trespasses" (Matt. 6:15).

II. Be Fervent
". . . fervent in spirit; serving the Lord" (Rom. 12:11).
- A. Fervent: "Having or showing great warmth of feeling; intensely devoted or earnest; ardent"—Webster.
- B. Some Christians do not serve the Lord fervently. They are lethargic and unexcited about the things of God.
- C. Being fervent in spirit is pleasing to God. Serve the Lord with joy and gladness and count it a privilege to be a member of the family of God (1 Peter 4:8).

III. Be Fruitful
"That ye might walk worthy of the Lord unto all pleasing, being fruitful in every good work . . ." (Col. 1:10).

A. Many Christians are slack when it comes to being fruitful for God, but they have plenty of time for their own concerns. They displease God.

B. According to Scripture, we are to be "filled with the fruits of righteousness ... unto the glory and praise of God" (Phil. 1:11).

C. The things we do for God count most and please him. They will bring everlasting rewards.

IV. Be Faithful

"Be thou faithful unto death, and I will give thee a crown of life" *(Rev. 2:10).*

A. Some people never miss work or exercise. They are faithful to everything that will benefit them materially and physically.

B. Many Christians are not as faithful to God's cause and kingdom as they are to their own interests. They displease the Lord.

C. Let us live so that someday we can hear him say, "Well done, thou good and faithful servant ... enter thou into the joy of thy lord" (Matt. 25:21).

12

"H-O-P-E Thou in God"

"Hope thou in God" (Ps. 42:5).

Hope is strengthened when we:

I. H-onor the Lord

"Now unto the King eternal, immortal, invisible, the only wise God, be honour and glory for ever and ever. Amen" (1 Tim. 1:17).

A. Many Christians fail to sufficiently honor God. They seek honor for themselves instead.

B. Scripture teaches: "How can ye believe, which receive honour one of another, and seek not the honour which cometh from God only?" (John 5:44).

C. We must give God all the glory and honor for what we have done, what we are doing, and what we will do. He is worthy. Our hope is in God. In time, he will give us the honor due us.

II. O-bey the Lord

"We ought to obey God rather than men" (Acts 5:29).

A. Peter and the other apostles were rebuked for preaching the gospel of Christ, but they stood fast and obeyed God.

B. Millions of people seek to please others rather than God. They are careless about many things—God's holy day, his tithe, their time, their talents, etc.

C. If our hope is in God, we must seek to please him. "That being justified by his grace, we should be made heirs according to the hope of eternal life" (Titus 3:7).

III. P-raise the Lord

"From the rising of the sun unto the going down of the same the LORD's name is to be praised" *(Ps. 113:3).*

A. Most Christians fail when it comes to praising the Lord. They forget, neglect, or are simply too busy with other things.

B. Let us make a determined effort to offer our praises to God. With the psalmist, we should endeavor to praise him continually. God is our hope (Ps. 34:1).

C. The text says, "Hope thou in God: for I shall yet praise him ..." (Ps. 42:5). "Happy is he ... whose hope is in the LORD his God" (Ps. 146:5).

IV. E-ndure for the Lord

"But he that shall endure unto the end, the same shall be saved" *(Matt. 24:13).*

A. Some Christians lack endurance. When trials and testings strike, they throw up their hands in despair.

B. We must be steadfast in the faith. "Holding fast the faithful word ..." (Titus 1:9). "In hope of eternal life, which God ... promised before the world began" (Titus 1:2).

13

How to Be a Successful Christian

"Rooted and built up in him, and stablished in the faith, as ye have been taught, abounding therein with thanksgiving" (Col. 2:7).

Everyone wants to be successful. The following points show us how to become successful Christians.

I. Be a Faithful Christian

"Be thou faithful unto death, and I will give thee a crown of life" (Rev. 2:10).

A. Faithful: "Firm in adherence to promises or in observance of duty"—Webster.

B. Many Christians are unsuccessful because they are not as faithful as they should be. They falter spiritually.

C. Some Christians are slack about their responsibilities and fail to keep promises. You can't depend on them, for you never know where to find them.

D. A successful Christian must be trustworthy with time, talent, and treasure. The Lord watches the faithful, and they will dwell with him eternally (Ps. 101:6).

II. Be a Hopeful Christian

"In hope of eternal life, which God, that cannot lie, promised before the world began" (Titus 1:2).

A. Hope is "desire accompanied by expectation of or belief in fulfillment"—Webster.

B. Today's world is filled with hopeless people who have no expectation of success. Some Christians fail to be hopeful also.

C. Christians know that man's only hope is in Jesus Christ.

They strive to bring others to a saving knowledge of him too.

D. To be a successful Christian one must hope in Christ, who is "the hope of eternal life" (Titus 3:7).

III. Be a Loving Christian

"Thou shalt love the Lord thy God with all thy heart . . . soul . . . strength . . . mind; and thy neighbour as thyself" (Luke 10:27).

A. In our world of hatred, terrorism, and destruction, Christians need to manifest love. For love "shall cover the multitude of sins" (1 Peter 4:8). It will influence others to accept Christ.

B. Some Christians live in strife and conflict. They fail in their quest to become loving Christians.

C. To be successful Christians we must be loving Christians. Scripture admonishes us to be "kindly affectioned one to another with brotherly love . . ." (Rom. 12:10).

D. The apostle Paul said, "And now abideth faith, hope, charity [love], these three; but the greatest of these is charity [love]" (1 Cor. 13:13).

14

How Christians Should P-R-A-Y

"Be careful for nothing; but in every thing by prayer and supplication with thanksgiving let your requests be made known unto God" (Phil. 4:6).

How should Christians P-R-A-Y? Here are some ways.

I. With P-raise
"Continue in prayer, and watch in the same with thanksgiving" (Col. 4:2).
   A. Many Christians do not praise the Lord adequately. They are anxious to receive from God but fail to praise him.
   B. We should begin all our prayers with praise to God. Thank him for his great love and mercy and the many blessings he bestows on us.
   C. The psalmist said, "I will bless the LORD at all times: his praise shall continually be in my mouth" (Ps. 34:1).

II. With R-egularity
"... men ought always to pray, and not to faint" (Luke 18:1).
   A. Many Christians hit and miss when it comes to their prayer life. When everything goes well, they neglect to pray. When tragedy strikes, they pray.
   B. We should continue in a spirit of prayer at all times, talking to God in good times as well as in bad times.
   C. Scripture admonishes Christians to "pray without ceasing" (1 Thess. 5:17).

III. With A-ssurance
"And this is the confidence that we have in him, that, if we ask any thing according to his will, he heareth us" (1 John 5:14).

A. Christians often fail to win the victory when they pray, because they lack faith.

B. James referred to the man whose faith wavered and said, "Let not that man think that he shall receive any thing of the Lord" (James 1:7).

C. We must pray with assurance. "And if we know that he hear us, whatsoever we ask, we know that we have the petitions that we desired of him" (1 John 5:15).

IV. With Y-ieldedness

"But yield yourselves unto God . . ." (Rom. 6:13).

A. In his most excruciating hour, Jesus prayed with yieldedness to his heavenly Father, "Nevertheless not as I will, but as thou wilt" (Matt. 26:39).

B. Many Christians today persist in having their own way. They forget that God's will is always best.

15

How God L-I-F-T-S His People

"I will extol thee, O LORD; for thou hast lifted me up ..." (Ps. 30:1).

God L-I-F-T-S his people today through the following ways.

I. L-oves Them

"... thou hast sent me, and hast loved them, as thou hast loved me" (John 17:23).

A. God loved us so much he gave his only Son to die on the cross for our sins.

B. God's love can lift the drunkard, thief, liar, prostitute, and homosexual out of the miry clay of sin (John 3:16).

C. We must come to God in faith, repent of our sins, and accept him as Savior and Lord.

II. I-nspires Them

"... hath begotten us again unto a lively hope ..." (1 Peter 1:3).

A. To inspire is "to influence, move, or guide by divine or supernatural inspiration"—Webster.

B. God inspires his people through prayer and the study of his Word. His Holy Spirit lifts them, giving them the hope of eternal life (Titus 1:2).

III. F-rees Them

"... where the Spirit of the Lord is, there is liberty" (2 Cor. 3:17).

A. Sin, self, and Satan bind many of God's people. Some are chained by the opinions of other people.

B. To be set free we must make a total commitment to the Lord. "If the Son therefore shall make you free, ye shall be free indeed" (John 8:36).

IV. T-ests Them

"That the trial of your faith, being much more precious than gold . . ." (1 Peter 1:7).

A. We must be patient and faithful during trials. God often lifts his people through testing and trials.

B. ". . . after that ye have suffered a while, make you perfect, stablish, strengthen, settle you" (1 Peter 5:10).

V. S-ecures Them

"To an inheritance incorruptible . . . reserved in heaven for you" (1 Peter 1:4).

A. Millions are seeking security by acquiring houses, land, silver, and gold, but they forget that temporal pursuits are fleeting.

B. Real and lasting security is found only in God. He lifts his people with a true security, a security that is eternal (2 Cor. 5:1).

16

How to H-A-V-E God's Best

"Call upon me, and I will answer thee, and shew thee great and mighty things, which thou knowest not" (Jer. 33:3).

I. H-ope for God's Best

"But I will hope continually, and will yet praise thee more and more" (Ps. 71:14).

A. The first step to having God's best is to hope for his best. Too many Christians settle for less.

B. God is pleased to give us his best, but we must desire to have it. We must ask, seek, and knock (Matt. 7:7).

C. The psalmist prayed, "Let thy mercy, O LORD, be upon us, according as we hope in thee" (Ps. 33:22).

II. A-im for God's Best

". . . forgetting those things which are behind, and reaching forth unto those things which are before" (Phil. 3:13).

A. Many Christians, and churches, do not aim high enough. They set their goals low because of their fear of failure.

B. We are not dependent on our own poor powers. We can do all things through Christ who strengthens us (Phil. 4:13).

C. We must aim for God's highest and best. Our strength is finite. God's power, on the other hand, is infinite. Depend on him.

III. V-isualize God's Best

"I will lift up mine eyes unto the hills, from whence cometh my help. My help cometh from the LORD . . ." (Ps. 121:1–2).

A. Some Christians do not visualize God's best. They settle for the lowlands of self-seeking and self-indulgence.

B. Paul received a vision of God's best. "To open their eyes, and to turn them from darkness to light. . . . I was not disobedient unto the heavenly vision" (Acts 26:18–19).

C. We must visualize God's best also. We must seek to turn the lost "from the power of Satan unto God," as Paul did.

IV. E-xpect God's Best

"Now faith is the substance of things hoped for, the evidence of things not seen" (Heb. 11:1).

A. When it comes to doing God's work, many Christians falter and fail. They forget, neglect, or simply refuse to accomplish much for God.

B. We cannot expect to have God's best unless we do our best. "Even so faith, if it hath not works, is dead, being alone" (James 2:17).

How to Live Victoriously

"But thanks be to God, which giveth us the victory through our Lord Jesus Christ" (1 Cor. 15:57).

Christians need to live victoriously. They should:

I. Live in God's Presence

"Surely the righteous shall give thanks unto thy name: the upright shall dwell in thy presence" (Ps. 140:13).

A. Many Christians fail to live in God's presence. Secular activities crowd out prayer and communication with God.

B. To live victoriously we must continue in a spirit of prayer and fellowship with God. Scripture admonishes, "Pray without ceasing" (1 Thess. 5:17).

II. Live by God's Promises

"Whereby are given unto us exceeding great and precious promises: that by these ye might be partakers of the divine nature . . ." (2 Peter 1:4).

A. Some Christians neglect the promises. They do not read, remember, and claim them as their own.

B. To be victorious we must live by the promises of God. They "were written . . . for our learning, that we through patience and comfort of the scriptures might have hope" (Rom. 15:4).

III. Live with God's Peace

"Peace I leave with you, my peace I give unto you . . ." (John 14:27).

A. Millions in today's world seek peace. They attain education, popularity, and wealth, but fail to find lasting peace.

B. Real and lasting peace is found only in Jesus Christ. His peace keeps our hearts and minds and helps us to live victoriously (Phil. 4:7).

IV. Live Through God's Power
"I can do all things through Christ which strengtheneth me" (Phil. 4:13).
A. When Christians try to get by on their own power, they fail. Finite power is insufficient for the challenges of our day.
B. We can live victoriously only through God's power. Through his power we can accomplish his work here on earth (Col. 1:10–11).

V. Live for God's Purpose
"According to the eternal purpose which he purposed in Christ Jesus our Lord" (Eph. 3:11).
A. When Christ died on the cross, he became our substitute because he paid for our sins and accomplished God's purpose. We must only repent and believe in him to receive salvation.
B. God has a purpose for each of us also. If we are to live victoriously, we must seek God's purpose. He has promised to direct each of us individually (Prov. 3:6).

18

Jesus Christ, the L-I-F-E

"Jesus saith unto him, I am the way, the truth, and the life: no man cometh unto the Father, but by me" (John 14:6).

Jesus Christ, the L-I-F-E, is the:

I. L-ifting Life

"I will extol thee, O LORD; for thou hast lifted me up . . ." (Ps. 30:1).

A. When Jesus was here on earth, he lifted the sick, suffering, and sinful (Mark 9:27). He brought life to those who were dead in trespasses and sins.

B. Jesus is the same today. He lifts the low—drunkards, drug abusers, liars, prostitutes, homosexuals—all who come to him and forsake their sins.

C. Christ paid the penalty for the sins of all mankind. We need only to repent and believe, and he will lift us out of the miry clay of sin (Acts 16:31).

II. I-ndwelling Life

"I will not leave you comfortless: I will come to you" (John 14:18).

A. When Christians surrender all to God, they are cleansed and filled with Christ's Holy Spirit (Acts 15:8–9).

B. Spirit-filled Christians are empowered to do service for God (Acts 1:8). Their delight is to work and witness, thus expanding God's kingdom here on earth.

C. Christ's Holy Spirit indwells the lives of totally committed Christians. They are never alone (John 14:16).

III. F-ulfilling Life

"For he satisfieth the longing soul, and filleth the hungry soul with goodness" (Ps. 107:9).

- A. Millions of people live unfulfilled lives. The longing in their souls is never satisfied.
- B. Many search for happiness by attaining possessions, seeking pleasure, and pursuing personal interests, but they fail to find real and lasting joy.
- C. Fulfillment is found only in Jesus Christ. We must accept him as Savior and Lord by giving him first place in our life (Matt. 6:33).

IV. E-verlasting Life

". . . that whosoever believeth in him should not perish, but have everlasting life" (John 3:16).

- A. Few things in this world are permanent. Our possessions rust, decay, are lost or destroyed. They soon vanish.
- B. Jesus said, "I am come that they might have life, and that they might have it more abundantly" (John 10:10).
- C. "Verily, verily, I say unto you, He that believeth on me hath everlasting life" (John 6:47).

19

Keeping Watch

"But I keep under my body, and bring it into subjection: lest that by any means, when I have preached to others, I myself should be a castaway" (1 Cor. 9:27).

I. Watch What You Think

". . . bringing into captivity every thought to the obedience of Christ" (2 Cor. 10:5).

A. Many Christians fail to bring their thoughts into captivity. They fall prey to evil and negative thinking and brooding.

B. We must replace evil and negative thoughts with good and positive ones, keeping our mind filled with that which is "pure" and "of good report" (Phil. 4:8).

II. Watch What You See

"But mine eyes are unto thee, O GOD the Lord (Ps. 141:8).

A. Millions of people are deceived by the scenes of illicit sex and destruction as displayed on television.

B. What would Jesus have us see? We must avoid exposure to the filth and violence that television and the movies propagate (Heb. 12:2).

III. Watch What You Hear

"He that heareth . . . and believeth . . . hath everlasting life" (John 5:24).

A. Today's world is flooded with suggestive music, foul language, slander, and smut.

B. We must listen to the Word of God and to the cries of the needy, lonely, discouraged, and lost (Rom. 10:17).

IV. Watch What You Say

"For by thy words thou shalt be justified, and by thy words thou shalt be condemned" (Matt. 12:37).

A. Many Christians are defeated by their own harsh, critical words. They fail to be the blessing they should be.

B. We must watch what we say. "A soft answer turneth away wrath: but grievous words stir up anger" (Prov. 15:1).

V. Watch What You Do

"... in every good work to do his will ..." (Heb. 13:21).

A. Some Christians default when it comes to God's work. They are too involved with personal pursuits.

B. We must make time for God. Give a smile, a kind word, a good deed. Lead others to Christ (1 Tim. 6:18–19).

VI. Watch Where You Go

"As ye have therefore received Christ Jesus the Lord, so walk ye in him" (Col. 2:6).

A. Many Christians go almost everywhere except for God. They try to satisfy the longing in their soul.

B. We must be faithful to the church, to calling on the sick, and to witnessing to the lost. When we go for God, he goes with us (Josh. 1:9).

20

Does It Pay
to Be a Faithful Christian?

"The faithful man shall abound with blessings" (Prov. 28:20).

How do faithful Christians experience God's rich blessings?

I. The Faithful Pray and Are Blessed
"And all things, whatsoever ye shall ask in prayer, believing, ye shall receive" (Matt. 21:22).

A. Most Christians fail to pray as much as they should. They forget or simply neglect to pray.

B. Prayer, plus faith, brings miracles. The promise is that "believing, ye shall receive" (Matt. 21:22).

C. We must pray more frequently. We are admonished to "pray without ceasing" (1 Thess. 5:17).

II. The Faithful Focus on the Promises and Are Blessed
"For whatsoever things were written aforetime were written for our learning . . ." (Rom. 15:4).

A. Some Christians are unable to appropriate God's promises because they feel excluded, but God's promises are for every individual who trusts in them.

B. God's Word assures us that the promises "were written for our learning, that we through patience and comfort of the scriptures might have hope" (Rom. 15:4).

C. Knowing and claiming the promises of God unlock the door to blessings and miracles galore. We must read, remember, and claim them.

III. The Faithful Are Patient and Are Blessed
"In your patience possess ye your souls" (Luke 21:19).

A. Many Christians lack patience. They want things to happen at their appointed time and place.
B. Patience opens the door to kindness, understanding, and Christlikeness.
C. James admonished, "But let patience have her perfect work, that ye may be perfect and entire, wanting nothing" (James 1:4).

IV. The Faithful Persevere and Are Blessed

"... after that ye have suffered a while, make you perfect ..." (1 Peter 5:10).

A. Some Christians give up too quickly. When they become discouraged, they throw up their hands in despair.
B. We should practice perseverance, to keep on when the going gets tough.
C. Perseverance opens the door to dependability and strength. "... stablish, strengthen, settle you" (1 Peter 5:10).

V. The Faithful Praise God and Are Blessed

"Great is the LORD, and greatly to be praised; and his greatness is unsearchable" (Ps. 145:3).

A. Most Christians fail when it comes to praising God. They are too busy coping with the stresses of life.
B. Praise enables us to handle the stresses that seem to bombard us. To praise, we must look at the positives. God is pleased when we praise him (Ps. 68:19).

21

"Let This Mind Be in You"

"Let this mind be in you, which was also in Christ Jesus" (Phil. 2:5).

What does it mean to possess the mind of Christ? It is to have:

I. A Prayerful Mind

". . . in everything by prayer and supplication with thanksgiving let your requests be made known unto God" (Phil. 4:6).

A. Some Christians fail to pray about everything. They wait until tragedy strikes to pray.

B. Jesus prayed about both the great and small. He kept himself in a spirit of prayer and often prayed alone for extended periods (Luke 6:12).

II. A Positive Mind

". . . whatsoever things are of good report . . . think on these things" (Phil. 4:8).

A. Many Christians think negatively. They dwell on gloom and expect the worst to happen. We must look for the good instead of the bad.

B. Jesus was a positive thinker. He possessed a positive faith. "If ye shall ask anything in my name," he told his disciples, "I will do it" (John 14:14).

III. A Patient Mind

"But let patience have her perfect work, that ye may be perfect and entire, wanting nothing" (James 1:4).

A. Jesus waits patiently for all who will come unto him (Rev. 3:20).

B. We must be patient, kind, and understanding, ready to lift the less fortunate and work to win the lost to him.

IV. A Peaceful Mind

"Peace I leave with you, my peace I give unto you . . ." (John 14:27).

A. Millions are searching for peace but fail to find it. Many Christians do not have the measure of peace they need.

B. Jesus promised to give peace to those who trust him. He admonished, "Let not your heart be troubled, neither let it be afraid" (John 14:27).

V. A Purposeful Mind

"Having made known unto us the mystery of his will, according to his good pleasure which he hath purposed in himself" (Eph. 1:9).

A. Many people live without purpose. They merely exist and are miserable and unhappy. To be successful we must live with a goal in mind.

B. Christ's life was vibrant with purpose. He came to earth on a mission. He lived, died, was resurrected, ascended, and is coming again with purpose (Eph. 3:11).

22

"Love One Another"

"A new commandment I give unto you, That ye love one another; as I have loved you, that ye also love one another. By this shall all men know that ye are my disciples, if ye have love one to another" (John 13:34–35).

Christians need to love God and others more. The following points describe the kind of love we need.

I. A Love that Shares
"A new commandment I give unto you, That ye love one another" (John 13:34).
A. Many Christians profess to love God and others but fail to share their time, talent, and treasure.
B. Some Christians are tight-fisted with God. They do not pay the tenth (tithe) of their earnings. They fail to give liberal offerings too.
C. To love God and others, we must share. Be ready to give a smile or a kind word, do something to help the needy, and share your testimony.
D. Scripture admonishes, "If a brother or sister be naked, and destitute of daily food and . . . ye give them not those things which are needful to the body; what doth it profit?" (James 2:15–16).

II. A Love that Sacrifices
". . . as I have loved you, that ye also love one another" (John 13:34).
A. Humankind sinned and deserved to die, but Christ loved us so much he took our place. He died on the cross for us.

B. The Bible says, "Because he laid down his life for us: we ought to lay down our lives for the brethren" (1 John 3:16).
C. Sacrifice is "a destruction or surrender of something for the sake of something else"—Webster.
D. Scripture admonishes, ". . . let us . . . love . . . in deed and in truth" (1 John 3:18).

III. A Love that Shows
"By this shall all men know that ye are my disciples, if ye have love one to another" (John 13:35).

A. Christians' love for God and others speaks louder than words. It shows when it is present and also when it is lacking.
B. Scripture says, "Let your light so shine before men, that they may see your good works, and glorify your Father which is in heaven" (Matt. 5:16).
C. Christians' light shines through their love for God and others. Love is attractive and needful.
D. Love is a psychological and spiritual need. Everyone needs to love and be loved. God's love cannot be hidden. It reaches outward to bless others and glorify him.

23

"Rivers of Living Water"

"He that believeth on me, as the scripture hath said, out of his belly shall flow rivers of living water" (John 7:38).

Water illustrates the work of the Holy Spirit. Christians need to lead Spirit-filled lives through which God's love can flow to others.

I. The In-flow
A. The Ohio, Arkansas, and Missouri Rivers flow into the Mississippi River, thus increasing its capacity and momentum.
B. Rivers of living water need inlets also. The inflow of prayer, Bible study, and fellowship with God's people are critical to our spiritual growth and development.
C. God's Word tells us: ". . . in every thing by prayer and supplication with thanksgiving let your requests be made known unto God" (Phil. 4:6).

II. The Out-flow
A. Rivers must have outlets. Outlets are necessary for their existence. The Dead Sea contains no life because it has no outflow.
B. Rivers of living water need outlets for their existence also. The outflow of the fruits of the Spirit are a blessing to others and bring glory to God.
C. "But the fruit of the Spirit is love, joy, peace, longsuffering, gentleness, goodness, faith, meekness, temperance: against such there is no law" (Gal. 5:22–23).

III. The Under-flow
A. The undercurrent flows beneath the surface of the river. Sin

is an undercurrent that is treacherous and dangerous. Christians must be on guard against it.

B. The underflow of living water is "the peace of God, which passeth all understanding..." (Phil. 4:7). It holds us steady and steadfast when the storms of life are raging.

C. God's Word promises, "When the enemy shall come in like a flood, the Spirit of the LORD shall lift up a standard against him" (Isa. 59:19).

IV. The Over-flow

A. The overflow of rivers brings enrichment to the soil along their banks. The crops yield an abundant and bountiful harvest.

B. The overflow of living water is the work of the Holy Spirit. "But this spake he of the Spirit . . ." (John 7:39). This spiritual overflow blesses lives, warms hearts, and revives spirits.

C. The overflow is attractive. Young and old, rich and poor, great and small, every one of God's children needs the inflow, outflow, underflow, and overflow of God's Spirit that the "rivers of living water" give.

24

Sowing and Reaping

"They that sow in tears shall reap in joy" (Ps. 126:5).

All Christians should desire to be better workers for the Lord. Here are some points to ponder.

I. The Preparing
"He that goeth forth and weepeth . . ." (Ps. 126:6).
   A. Many Christians do not make proper preparations for accomplishing God's work. They rely on their own insufficient powers and fail.
   B. To accomplish God's work successfully requires a concern. A feeling of urgency is needed.
   C. We must be prayerful, claim God's promises, and depend on God's power to work through us. Our power is finite; God's power is infinite and never fails.

II. The Planting
". . . bearing precious seed . . ." (Ps. 126:6).
   A. Some Christians fail in their use of God's Word. They rely on their own words. This produces failure.
   B. "The seed is the word of God" (Luke 8:11). Plant it faithfully with the assurance that God's Word "shall not return unto me void . . ." (Isa. 55:11).
   C. Successful workers use the Word of God. They memorize it, know where key texts are found, and dispense it generously, trusting God for the results (Luke 8:15).

III. The Praising
". . . shall doubtless come again with rejoicing . . ." (Ps. 126:6).

A. Most Christians need to praise the Lord more. They lose many blessings because of a failure to do so.

B. We should praise the Lord for what he has done, for what he is doing, and for what he will do.

C. When we see God's work accomplished, we should praise him. The psalmist said, "His praise shall continually be in my mouth" (Ps. 34:1).

IV. The Presenting

". . . bringing his sheaves with him" (Ps. 126:6).

A. Too many Christians want credit and honor for themselves.

B. We must give God all the glory and honor for what we have accomplished. Paul said, "Whatsoever ye do, do all to the glory of God" (1 Cor. 10:31).

C. If we are faithful in this life, we shall hear the Lord say, "Well done, thou good and faithful servant" (Matt. 25:21) when we present our sheaves to him in the next life.

25

The Christian's Conquest

"The steps of a good man are ordered by the LORD: and he delighteth in his way. Though he fall, he shall not be utterly cast down: for the LORD upholdeth him with his hand" (Ps. 37:23–24).

The Christian life is one of conquest. This includes:

I. The Directing
"The steps of a good man are ordered by the LORD . . ." (Ps. 37:23).
- A. Many Christians do not depend on God for direction. They go their own way, follow their own desires, and fail.
- B. To receive God's direction, we must pray, consult God's Word, and trust him to lead us in his way.
- C. Scripture admonishes, "In all thy ways acknowledge him, and he shall direct thy paths" (Prov. 3:6).

II. The Delighting
"And he delighteth in his way" (Ps. 37:23).
- A. God is pleased when we seek his guidance, his direction, for our lives.
- B. We must seek to please God and "be delighted in his way" because his will and way are always best.
- C. The psalmist wrote, "I delight to do thy will, O my God: yea, thy law is within my heart" (Ps. 40:8).

III. The Downfall
"Though he fall, he shall not be utterly cast down" (Ps. 37:24).
- A. No one is perfect. We all make mistakes, blunders, and fail at times, but God is merciful and patient.
- B. All Christians fall into trouble, difficulties, sorrow, sick-

ness, and suffering at one time or another. God will not allow us to "be utterly cast down."

C. The psalmist said, "Cast thy burdens upon the LORD, and he shall sustain thee: he shall never suffer the righteous to be moved" (Ps. 55:22).

IV. The Deliverance

"For the LORD upholdeth him with his hand" (Ps. 37:24).

A. Some Christians fail to sufficiently trust God for deliverance. They continue to live in desperation.

B. God has promised to sustain us in our afflictions and distresses, and he will deliver those who trust in him.

C. God's Word promises, "And the LORD shall help them, and deliver them . . . and save them, because they trust in him" (Ps. 37:40).

26

"These Three" Set You Free

"And now abideth faith, hope, charity [love], these three; but the greatest of these is charity [love]" (1 Cor. 13:13).

The following points describe the kind of faith, hope, and love we need today.

I. Faith that Dares

"And now abideth faith . . ." (1 Cor. 13:13).

- A. Many Christians are lacking in faith that dares. Their faith is complacent, inactive, and fails to accomplish things for God.
- B. Faith that dares is faith that is active. Scriptures teach that "faith, if it hath not works, is dead, being alone" (James 2:17).
- C. Active faith sets us free from the bondage of sin, Satan, and self. It believes God and acts on his promises.
- D. Faith that dares works for us as we work our faith.

II. Hope that Cares

"And now abideth . . . hope . . ." (1 Cor. 13:13).

- A. Many build their hopes on temporal pursuits—accumulating real estate, bank accounts, and gadgets galore. These will soon vanish away.
- B. In today's society many possess a self-centered hope. It fails to care about God and others. This hope will not endure.
- C. We must have hope that involves the less fortunate, the elderly, the helpless, and the homeless. This hope is built on Jesus Christ and will endure eternally.

D. "Which hope we have as an anchor of the soul, both sure and stedfast . . ." (Heb. 6:19).

III. Love that Shares

"And now abideth . . . charity [love] . . ." (1 Cor. 13:13).

A. Many Christians are selfish. They fail to love God and others as they should.

B. God shared his love when he gave Jesus to die on the cross for our sins (John 3:16). Jesus shared his life and love by paying the penalty for our sins.

C. We must possess a love that shares also. Our love must be ready to give a lift to those who are homeless and hungry, or discouraged and depressed.

D. Faith is needful; hope is necessary; but love is a must. Love is eternal. ". . . God is love . . ." (1 John 4:16). ". . . the greatest of these is charity [love]" (1 Cor. 13:13).

27

When You Are Under Pressure

"Casting all your care upon him; for he careth for you" (1 Peter 5:7).

I. Expand Your Thinking of God
"Thou wilt keep him in perfect peace, whose mind is stayed on thee . . ." (Isa. 26:3).
   A. Many Christians fail to keep their mind on the Lord. They allow evil thoughts to linger. These bring them into bondage.
   B. We must replace evil and negative thoughts with good and positive ones (Phil. 2:5).

II. Expand Your Looking to God
"Looking unto Jesus the author . . . of our faith" (Heb. 12:2).
   A. Some Christians see only the faults and failures in others. They look for the bad in circumstances.
   B. We must strive to see the good in others and in our circumstances. We must keep our eyes on Jesus. He never fails.

III. Expand Your Hearing from God
"Incline your ear . . . hear, and your soul shall live" (Isa. 55:3).
   A. The Lord speaks to those who listen. He speaks through prayer, his Word, and the Holy Spirit. ". . . faith cometh by hearing . . ." (Rom. 10:17).
   B. Despite the pressures of life, we must take time to hear from God. He often speaks in a "still small voice."

IV. Expand Your Talking About God
"Talk ye of all his wondrous works" (Ps. 105:2).

A. Most Christians talk about the news and their neighbors. They talk about everything except the Lord.
B. We should talk about the goodness and greatness of God. He renews, revives, and releases us from the pressures of daily living.

V. Expand Your Doing for God
". . . in every good work to do his will . . ." (Heb. 13:21).
A. Many Christians are too busy with personal pursuits. They neglect to accomplish God's work.
B. We should expand our doing for God. Give a smile and a kind word, or do a good deed. God will be glorified; others will be encouraged; and you will be blessed.

VI. Expand Your Going with God
". . . we walk by faith, not by sight" (2 Cor. 5:7).
A. Almost everyone is on the go. We must go more for God.
B. Be faithful in church attendance. Visit the lonely and elderly. Witness to the lost and bring the unchurched to him.

28

"Where Is Your Faith?"

"And he said unto them, Where is your faith?" (Luke 8:25).

Most people have a measure of faith, but it makes a vast difference in whom or what we put our faith. "Where is your faith?"

I. In Popularity?
"How can ye believe, which receive honour one of another ..." (John 5:44).
- A. Many people put their faith in popularity. They desire to receive honor from others at any cost.
- B. We must seek the honor that God gives. His honor is eternal. We need to humble ourselves before God, "... that he may exalt you in due time" (1 Peter 5:6).

II. In Pleasure?
"Ye have lived in pleasure on the earth, and been wanton" (James 5:5).
- A. Millions love pleasure more than God. They live for fun and entertainment. Their pleasure is fleeting at best (2 Tim. 3:4).
- B. The pleasure that Christ gives is lasting. Christians are forgiven, cleansed, and on their way to heaven. There they shall receive God's eternal pleasures (Ps. 16:11).

III. In Position?
"Labour not for the meat which perisheth, but for that meat which endureth unto everlasting life ..." (John 6:27).
- A. Many people put their faith in their job or social position. They live for temporal pursuits.
- B. We must give God first place, seeking to please him (Matt.

6:33). Attend God's house, visit the sick and elderly, assist the needy, and witness to the lost.

IV. In Possessions?

". . . a man's life consisteth not in . . . the things which he possesseth" (Luke 12:15).

A. Millions put their faith in possessions. They love money, houses, cars, and gadgets more than they love God.

B. Scripture warns us not to "trust in uncertain riches, but in the living God, who giveth us richly all things to enjoy" (1 Tim. 6:17).

V. In People?

"And Jesus answering saith unto them, Have faith in God" (Mark 11:22).

A. Some people put their faith in doctors, lawyers, preachers, and friends. They come to disappointment.

B. While we should appreciate the good we receive from others, our ultimate faith, trust, and dependence must be in God. His power is unlimited and never fails (2 Tim. 1:12).